In My Pain – Strength Is Not Optional

By

Chennetta Renae

Printed in the United States of America

First Edition, 2023

HARDBACK ISBN 978-1-0880-8210-2
PAPERBACK ISBN 978-1-0880-8203-4
EBOOK ISBN 978-1-0880-8207-2

Red Pen Edits and Consulting

www.redpeneditsllc.com

TABLE OF CONTENTS

ACKNOWLEDGMENTS

First and foremost, I want to thank God for granting me the strength and courage to persevere in completing this project, which was a long and arduous undertaking.

I want to give a very special thanks to Torre A. Stocker of Red Pen Edits and Consulting, LLC for working diligently with me on this book. Thank you for all of your time in reading, editing, and helping to format my manuscript. Your contributions helped to make this book what it has become. I am most appreciative of your kindness, support, and patience throughout this entire process.

I want to thank my parents, Roderick and Cynthia McQueen

Thank you for your unconditional love and support throughout my life and this process.

Mommy - your prayers, encouragement and strength have kept me in awe. You are the strongest woman I know.

Daddy, the first man to have my heart - you are a quiet storm and my ultimate protector.

I LOVE YOU BOTH IMMENSELY.

To my beautiful sisters and my handsome brothers

Your big sister loves you all like crazy.

To my nieces and nephews

Auntie loves you the most.

I am thankful for those in my life who gave encouragement throughout this process and pushed me to completion. Your support is greatly appreciated. I'm thankful for those who have crossed my path over the years and impacted my life substantially.

To my king, my wonderful husband, Javonne P. Scott, Sr.

Your continuous, steadfast support and love are everything. Thank you for always protecting and supporting me. When I wanted to give up, you wouldn't let me. For that, I am grateful. I'm thankful for the way that you love me. This is forever! #143

Last but certainly not least of all, I want to thank my **children - Destenee (Des), Javonne Jr. (LJ), Cassandra (Cassie) and Savannah (Vannah)**. They have been some of my biggest supporters during this process. They often encouraged me to take time to write and would make sure that they didn't disturb me. Oftentimes, they would check on me and bring me water and snacks. You all are mommy's biggest reasons for living. You bring me immeasurable joy and unconditional love. I am blessed and honored to have been chosen to be your mommy.

DEDICATION

To my husband, Jay, who is my superman your love and support is immeasurable.

You are the love of my life. I will never be able to thank you enough for all that you have been for me. Thank you for continually choosing to love me. #143

To my heartbeats Destenee (Des), Javonne Jr. (LJ), Cassandra (Cassie) and Savannah (Vannah)

Thank you for giving me four more reasons to LIVE. You are the light of my world!

I LOVE YOU ALL TO LIFE!

CHAPTER 1

Introduction/ Testimony

I was born in Paterson, NJ on Monday, December 19, 1977, at 7:45 pm. I was raised by my father and mother. I am the oldest of 5. My childhood was good, but my parents were strict. I would later in life find out why that was but growing up, I didn't understand. In New Jersey, we were surrounded by family, and I loved it there. I have very fond memories of my childhood in New Jersey. That would all change after the passing of my paternal grandmother in August of 1988. My parents decided to relocate to Aynor, SC on October 13, 1990. We were raised in the church and there were lots of things, as "Christians", we were unable to do or participate in. I was unable to date until my senior year in high school. The few dates that I was allowed to go on, except for the last two I went on before leaving for the Army, I had to take one of my sisters with me. We were told to not have sex until marriage and like most teens I didn't abide by that losing my virginity at the age of 16. I decided to have sex for the first time with a young man who I thought I was in love with despite not being able to "have a boyfriend". We started out Baptist, attending what we referred to as the family church, Grace Chapel. I have family members from both sides who still attend and hold positions in that church. My grandmother's funeral was held there as well as my parents' wedding. My parents then joined Reformed Church of God which was pastored by my father's best friend's dad. Once we moved to SC, we joined another family church, St. Elizabeth Baptist. Then, in 1992, we joined Miracle Tabernacle of Prayer which was a Holiness church. In addition to all the things we were told as Baptist at this church, it was taught that women didn't wear pants or makeup. I wanted to be like the other girls. I wanted to wear jeans and shorts, especially in the colder months. I would sneak and wear them. I would also sneak and wear eyeliner and lipstick. It was while attending one of those churches that I would have my first encounter with a sexual predator. We will call him elder care bear in disguise. He appeared to be very nice and charming but would turn out to be sick and twisted. It didn't start immediately. It was gradual after a year or so of our family attending the church. He would say inappropriate things and would try to touch you. He always wanted one of the girls to sit in the front seat with him in his car because he would often take the teenagers at the church to different places. He was a first-class creep. I once enjoyed being around him until he showed his true colors and after that all I wanted to do was get away from him as fast as I could. I felt guilty when I graduated and finally left home because I felt like I left my sisters to fall victim to him. Years later, it would be revealed that he impregnated a girl, and his secret was out. Everybody now knew who he truly was. My sisters and I never told my parents. Honestly, we didn't think they would believe us. Especially since as teenage girls, we had sometimes been disobedient and broken rules. Our parents thought highly of this man as did all the other adults who he had fooled. The teenagers all knew what was up and talked amongst ourselves about him as we tried to ensure that we kept our distance when possible. This was my first experience with someone in a leadership position being inappropriate with me and not feeling like I could tell anyone about it.

I almost gave up, but I am thankful that I wasn't successful. On Sunday, September 15th, 2019, I requested that my Pastor pray for me. I got a breakthrough that was a long time coming. It was the beginning of my healing process. You see, I wanted to give up. I have had lots of suicidal thoughts in the past and even tried giving up twice by way of suicide. Thank God neither of my attempts were successful. At the age of 18, while serving in the Army, I was raped. I was repeatedly raped by one of my drill sergeants during Basic Training. I was also raped by 2 other men during my time in service. Until recently, I could not even speak those words. I had only told my husband. My parents did not even know until recently. I blamed myself. I felt like I must have had victim etched on my forehead or something that caused those men to be drawn to me. I always desired to be a daddy's girl. I longed for that relationship. I was what some would deem boy crazy in that I liked…. No, I loved boys. I would flirt but it rarely went past flirting. I just wanted to know that boys thought I was pretty. I used to wear glasses and had braces and I didn't always feel attractive. So, by my senior year, when I was no longer wearing braces or glasses, I had built up some confidence and thought I was pretty. But deep down I still wanted to know that others thought that too, besides my mommy.

CHAPTER 2

Basic Training

I graduated at the age of 17 and although I had a scholarship offer to go to Winthrop, I felt like that wasn't far enough to get out of my parent's strict grasp and that my dad could easily drive there anytime he wanted. With that, I decided to take the business card of one of the recruiters who had visited my school many times just to see what he had to offer. I took the ASVAB. It's like a placement test for the military and I scored high. I was excited and had no idea that my recruiter had a quota to meet as he "helped" me pick my MOS. He came to my home to speak with my parents, and they had to both sign for me to be able to enlist. Arriving at Fort Jackson (South Carolina) was more frightening than exciting. I wanted to be excited. I was finally leaving my parent's house and would be able to experience some things that I thought I was missing out on by being under their roof. Just the night before, I was partying by the pool at the hotel in Columbia, SC that they put me in with the 20 other recruits that got picked up along my route to start our new journey as enlistees in the United States Army. I was picked up at 2am as my family slept. I sat in the dark on the couch in the living room waiting for the van that would pick me up to arrive. My house was the 1st stop on the trip from Galivants Ferry, SC to Fort Jackson, SC.

The next day, I was picked up from the hotel to go to Reception as it is called when you arrive on the base for Basic Training. I, along with 100s of others, were greeted by a sea of buses that we were loaded onto to be taken to the barracks where we would stay until assigned to our Basic Training Unit. We loaded the buses and rode a short distance before arriving at the reception barracks and lots of yelling Drill Sergeants. I was not afraid of them, but I was nervous of what this new experience would entail. I heard my father's stories of being in the Marines. In high school, I was active. I ran track, was a member of the dance team, and a member of the JROTC program. My father had also been making me run 2 miles with him daily. I got off the bus, gathered my things and made my way to one of the many lines that were forming as they instructed us where to go. My father was a Veteran. He had served in the Marines, so the yelling didn't faze me. I had been prepared mentally for this. I felt confident that I could handle all that would be thrown my way. Due to my time in JROTC in high school and a letter from my Colonel I entered basic training with the rank of E2, a Private 2nd Class.

The first night there was chill. I was missing my parents and siblings, but they took us to a basketball game, and we were fed pizza and popcorn (I guess they were showing us one last good time before introducing us to our new hell). I was assigned to Company A, 1st Battalion, 61st Infantry Regiment 2nd Platoon. Each unit had 2 drill sergeants assigned to them. The first one we will call DS Payne because he reminded me of Damon Wayan's character, Major Payne. The other drill sergeant, I will refer to as DS Predator.

During Basic Training, we are required to have shifts on duty; either fire guard or charge of quarters (CQ). One night, I had been assigned to fire guard duty with another female. It was late at night, and we were sitting at the duty desk counting down until our shift would be over. DS Predator bought us pizza. That was against the rules, but we didn't care it was a treat and we weren't going to tell anyone. He told me to come with him. As I followed him through the boy's barracks to his office, I remembered feeling nervous. I was thinking that I was in trouble for something, however, I had no clue what it could be for. As we entered the office, I looked around and he told me to sit down. It was dark except for the light coming from the lamp on his desk. The office smelled good like his cologne. I recall wondering what brand it was. As I sat on the couch, my palms got sweaty, and I had a nervous feeling in my stomach. He came over to where I was sitting and asked me about my son. I told him that I didn't have a son. Someone started a rumor that I had a son. I assumed it was because I had pictures of my baby brother in my wall locker or because I talked about him all the time but yeah, the rumor was started. It wasn't the first time I had heard this. Back in the little town of Aynor, SC where my family and I resided, that rumor had also churned there. My brother is adopted and someone in town started the rumor that my parents adopted my son after I had gone off and had the baby. Meanwhile, I never gained any weight and most importantly never left town. So, when could I have been pregnant, let alone, given birth? I explained to DS Predator that, no, I do not have a son. He is my baby brother who I adore. He asked me was I a virgin and I said no that I was not but assured him that I was not a mother. I think the rumor had him believing that I was fast, an easy target. He told me that I was beautiful. I smiled and said thank you. I admit it. I liked getting compliments and was thinking he is nice and hand-some; maybe he picked up on that. The compliment put me at ease, and I no longer thought that I was in trouble although I was still unsure why I was in his office. He put his hand on my leg and I moved. I was so confused. Why did he have me in his office and why was he touching me? It didn't yet dawn on me what he was trying to do. I was so naive. He told me that it was ok and that I didn't have to be afraid. He liked me. At this point I was so nervous thinking about what was about to happen. He touched my arm. I moved again and asked to go back to the duty desk. He said no. He wasn't done with me yet. Before I could ask what that meant, he kissed me. I tried to stand up and he pushed me back down. I asked him what he was doing, and he said that he knew that I liked him and that I was a flirt. I had heard this a lot over the years and that I was a tease. I wondered when I had teased or flirted with him, but I knew that I hadn't. He and the other drill sergeant had been picking on me calling me NJ. I assume because I was born in NJ and carried that sort of swag with me, I guess. They were always picking on me, but I didn't think anything of it because this was basic training and my dad being a Marine, had already begun schooling me on what Basic Training entailed. Their job was to break us. Having been in ROTC, it came with the territory.

Next thing I know, he was on me. Although I was taller, he was much stronger. He was so strong. He was trying to remove my uniform pants and I remember thinking how I was taller than him, but he was so much stronger than me. I asked him to stop, but he wouldn't. I froze. I couldn't fight him. I couldn't scream, I couldn't do anything. His office was inside the boy's barracks. Why didn't I scream for help? I still can't answer that question. I just laid there. I started to cry while asking him to stop and telling him no, but he proceeded to rape me. It felt like it lasted for an eternity as I laid there crying, but it was only about 10 minutes or so. When he was done, he told me to get dressed and go back to duty like nothing happened. I instantly tried to forget and think about something else as I took my seat beside the other female at the duty desk. Later when I was alone, I cried as I showered him off me. At PT the next morning, he winked and smiled at me. I remember feeling sick to my stomach and being so upset, confused, and scared. I felt lost and I didn't know who to tell or who could/would help me, so I remained silent. He continued to pick on me making me do pushups and other things out of the blue for no reason, which again, wasn't odd it was Basic Training after all.

I noticed I had duty more often. Each time, he would make me go to his office and rape me all over again. Sometimes, I wouldn't even have duty. I would be in my bunk sleeping. He would wake me up and make me go to his office. He started sending me letters and cards in the mail scented with his cologne. We would all sit around for mail call, and I would have 2 or more cards from him every other day with the scent of his cologne sprayed on it. Someone may be reading this saying to themselves, why did she keep going with him? I couldn't tell him no. He was in a leadership position. I was a new trainee who was still learning the ropes about my new environment. I was afraid and didn't know who I could turn to, so I continued to do as I was told. I look back now and think of all the things I could have done or wish I would have done. Hindsight is 20/20. If I had known then, what I know now, I am confident that I would have handled things differently. I didn't know what I didn't know as an 18-year-old. Years later, I would surmise that because I longed to be a daddy's girl and wasn't that, maybe subconsciously, I was attracting this unwanted attention. Before he raped me, I did think this man was handsome, but I never wanted this. I was raped weekly until around 2 weeks before we graduated from Basic Training. In a place where I should have been safe and protected while learning how to defend and protect my country, I was violated.

CHAPTER 3

Rape

The 2nd rape took place in the barracks where I was stationed at Fort Stewart in Georgia. I was now the mother of a baby girl and living off base. Although I no longer resided in the barracks, there were people that I associated with while living there who still lived there. One night I was invited to come hang out and although I had been raped in Basic Training, I hadn't become the woman that mistrusted all men, so I went. I got to the little kickback and was having a good time. I ate some food and had some drinks. By now, I was comfortable at my duty station and often hung out on the weekends before getting pregnant and having my daughter in July of 1996. After having her, I did hang out, but it wasn't every weekend. I was in a relationship and engaged to the man who is now my husband. He was currently stationed in Korea. So, at the party it was getting late. There were only a few of us left. I was one of 2 girls still there. The other girl and one of the guys, both unknown to me, left the room and I was alone with the guy whose room it was. I wouldn't say we were friends, but we were friendly, and I had known of him for months at this point. We were talking and laughing, and I got up to leave. He asked me not to go. I told him that I had to leave. I needed to go pick up my daughter from my neighbor who would babysit for me from time to time and then, go home. He grabbed my arm and I pulled away from him. I used an expletive asking him what he grabbed me for. He grabbed me again and we began to fight. I found myself in another situation where I was dealing with someone who made up in his mind that he was going to take something from me and was much stronger than me. He knocked me on to the bed and forcibly raped me. In therapy, they often asked me to describe the rape that was the worst or had the greatest impact. I would always go back to the first one because he was in a position of power and leadership. The 2nd rape was the worst in terms of pain. I was beaten up and raped. When he was done with me, I ran out of there as fast as I could. I wasn't even fully dressed when I made it to my car. I finished getting dressed in the parking lot in my car. I drove home in a daze. I couldn't believe it happened to me again. I had been taken advantage of by a "nice guy" ..... again. I have always been attracted to the "bad" guys per se. You know the kind of guys that were kind of hard but wouldn't hurt you, but you knew could handle themselves in a fight and had that sort of tough guy swag about them. When I thought about rape, I always thought it would be ugly guys who couldn't get girls to pay them any attention or guys who treated women badly, but I never expected nice guys to behave that way. Months prior to this incident, I had suffered my first miscarriage and was going through it alone because my fiancé was in Korea. Although I told him and we were both grieving, we were having to do it without each other for comfort because of the distance. It was a Friday night in 1998. I was in the bathroom getting ready to go to the club. I suddenly felt a sharp stabbing pain in my stomach as I sat on the toilet. I noticed I wasn't urinating. I was bleeding heavily and thought at the time that I was passing a huge blood clot. I quickly realized that I had just had a miscarriage. Until that moment, I didn't even know that I was pregnant. My daughter, Destenee, wasn't even a year old yet. I cleaned myself up, took a shower, and still went out. That next day, I felt horrible and called Jay in Korea to let him know what happened. After that call, I was so sad. I tried to kill myself by taking pills. I ended up having to have my stomach pumped. It was the 2nd worse thing I have ever experienced at the time. I do not recommend it.

The 3rd rape was by another person in leadership over me. He was a SFC in our platoon. We will call him SFC bulldog. When I looked at him that is what I was reminded. His head was huge just like a bulldog. I didn't care for him almost since our very first meeting. In July of 1997, I gave birth to my daughter Destenee. I was told by several male NCO's that if the Army wanted me to have a child, they would have issued me one. After I returned to work from maternity leave, a lot of the men in my unit made several nasty comments towards me. I did my best to ignore them. I quickly realized that I had joined a boy's club full of misogynistic men. SFC bulldog was the worst because he tried to pretend to be nice until he could no longer hide behind his mask. Under the guise that he was giving me a ride, he made a stop at his home. He made me get out of the car. I know you may be saying to yourself, she has already been raped by two other men why would she go with another one. Again, I was in a position where I was doing what I was told by leadership. You do as your told. You don't say no. Although I had been raped before, I had no idea that this was his intentions for me on that day until it was too late. So here I was again in a very vulnerable position with someone who was physically stronger than me. When he attacked me, all I could do was cry and beg him to please not do this. He talked about the clothes that I wore during off time and how I was flaunting around everybody. He stated that he deserved to get a sample of what I was already giving to SGT Scott. SGT Scott, Javonne Scott, is my husband, who at the time was my fiancé. Most people didn't know that. They did know that we were seeing each other. SFC bulldog didn't respect me and after raping me in his home that he shared with his wife and children I realized that it wasn't just me that he had no respect for. He was overconfident and not concerned about being found out.

During the moments when I was being raped, I was so scared that I never said anything after pleading with them to stop and saying no.

I, like most women of rape, have been asked "why didn't you report?" This is a victim blaming question. In Basic Training, the environment was new. I didn't know who I could tell or who would help. I didn't even know how the chain of command worked. Not only that, the 2nd drill sergeant assigned to my unit didn't rape me, but he often made inappropriate sexual comments and touched me inappropriately. I knew I couldn't go to him. He was later convicted of 3 counts of indecent assault; two counts of obstructing justice; one count of adultery, assault and attempted indecent assault as well as seven counts of disobeying orders. I was one of 8 females for whom he had been accused of sexual assault. I was asked why I didn't talk about my own incident when speaking about him. Well, I hadn't spoke about his inappropriate behavior with me. Someone else witnessed what he had done to me. When they reported what he had done to them, they included my name. I was not aware of any of this until after I got to my duty station in Fort Stewart, GA and was notified that I was being called to testify at Fort Jackson against him. This was a year or so later. It never dawned on me to bring up my rape during his trial to tell anyone about what happened to me at the hands of his coworker.

During my second rape I never told because I was ashamed. I blamed myself just like I had done previously but even more so because I had gone to the barracks where I no longer lived to visit with someone. Had I not gone there, it would not have happened. So instead, I went home, cleaned myself up, cried and drank myself to sleep. I went on like nothing happened.

I did report the 3rd rape to my female commander, who in return did absolutely nothing. I requested to be moved out of the platoon because he was a senior NCO, and she didn't even do that. I didn't think to go to the MPs or anyone else for that matter once she neglected to help me.

I want to remind everyone reading this that the causes of rape are not based on a female's actions. It's not based on her choice of clothing such as short skirts. It's not based on any impairment even if she may have consumed alcohol even to the point of drunkenness. It's not her flirty behavior, her promiscuous past, or being alone at night or anything that you can think of to blame the victim.

The ONLY cause of rape is the RAPIST!

I once read a story about a young lady walking home, and she took a shortcut. She saw a man who looked as if he was waiting for someone. She became afraid and said a prayer asking God to keep her safe and unharmed as she walked past the man. Later that day, as she sat in her home watching the news, she saw that the man she passed on the street had murdered and raped a young girl. The police said that the man told them that another girl had passed through the alley 10 minutes before and when asked why he didn't attack her, he said there was a man walking beside her. I used to question God, asking why he didn't protect me? I used to think it was because he was punishing me. I thought that I was being punished because my parents raised me and my siblings in church and I had strayed from what I had been taught.

Years later, I would hear someone say that we do not go through trials just for ourselves but for others. Even after hearing that, I still asked God why? I still do not have the answer. I have come to terms with the possibility that I will never know the answer. When it first happened, I questioned God all the time and by the time the 3rd guy raped me, I was angrily asking God why he would allow this to happen to me and where was He. I felt like the one guy repeatedly raping me was enough. Did I really have to endure two more men?

CHAPTER 4

Alcohol, Drugs and Suicide

I had no coping mechanisms before therapy. I turned to drugs and alcohol in an attempt to escape all the negative feelings that I have about what had happened to me, I had become so weak. I mainly drank. The only drug I have ever had/tried is weed. I smoked weed to help with the physical pain that I dealt with but the high also helped with the emotional pain. Weed and alcohol were temporary bandages and did little to cover my gashing wounds.

Back in 1997, I tried to kill myself and was taken to the hospital to have my stomach pumped. I had taken lots of pills. To this day, it is hard for me to take medicine.

In 2000, I tried to slit my wrists, but Jay walked in and stopped me.

On September 24, 2021, I was feeling the

lowest I had felt in years and almost committed suicide. Once again, I was going to take some pills. I was in my bathroom with the lights off standing in front of the sink when my youngest daughter Savannah came in and hugged my leg. I was crying and she said, "mommy it's going to be ok and hugged me tighter." Instead of taking the pills, I went in my bedroom and laid down with her and went to sleep.

I deal with overwhelming shame and guilt. Drinking seemed like the answer for me especially when being overtaken with intrusive thoughts and memories. I would do anything to forget. Being unable to sleep because of recurring dreams/nightmares, I would often drink just so I could go to sleep. I didn't realize that drinking would also mess with my sleep. I am thankful that although I chose to drink, I controlled my consumption and didn't become addicted. I did go from being an occasional drinker (having a few drinks a year) to having drinks with friends when we would hang out. Even in this, I chose to not consume much alcohol in a year's time. At one time, I was having a drink nightly for some months. The most I would consume would be 1 – 3 drinks a night. After doing this for months,

I worried that I could possibly cause damage to my liver. I stopped and chose instead to have a glass of wine occasionally.

CHAPTER 5

Promiscuity

After basic training, you go to AIT and while there, I began started wildin' out. I was living my best "hoe life!" What I didn't know at the time was that I was dealing with promiscuous behavior due to my sexual trauma. After basic training, I felt like damaged goods. I didn't care and all I knew was that from now on, things would be on my terms. I was having a lot of sex, but only on my terms. I was sleeping with different guys, and I didn't care. I was on a decline. I felt like I was in control of things and having sex on my terms ONLY or so I thought [Refer to 2nd and 3rd rape]. In AIT, I had one of the guys I was sleeping with shining my boots. I had other men doing things for me as well because I flirted with them. They probably thought I would sleep with them as well. Although I was out of control, I was still careful and selective. I only dealt with 2 guys during AIT, but I was sleeping with both of them at the same time.

The shame of rape will have you out here living wildly. I believe that my third rapist raped me because of who I was in a relationship with but also because of the people he had heard rumors of me sleeping with.

> I don't care if a woman has had a hundred sexual partners. Her yes to them is not an automatic yes to anyone else.

It is a woman's right, just as it is a man's right, to say no to whomever she chooses to say no to even after she says yes. We have the right to change our minds at any time! It is NO unless it is an unequivocal YES.

I have spent decades with self-blame, guilt, shame, self-doubt, and an immense decrease to my self-esteem. I had no self-worth. I was suicidal and I just didn't care. I had no thoughts about my future because I didn't see a positive future for myself. I felt hopeless.

I knew I was beautiful, and I loved my body,

but all of that changed. I used to be able to fall asleep minutes after my head hit the pillow. Now, I am unable to sleep most nights. I have developed physical health problems due to being raped and contracting chlamydia which led to my infertility issues. Even in all of that, God was working. In those same moments, I did not know it. I miscarried every child my husband and I conceived which totaled three. It was prophesied that my husband and I would conceive a son which was our desire.

When my fiancé was in Korea, we had racked up an expensive phone bill and I was unable to speak with him on the phone like we had been doing and letters were not coming quickly enough. I was lonely and still dealing with the grief of miscarriage and unknowingly my rapes. I didn't know back then how not seeking help after being raped was impairing my judgement and thinking. I began to have an affair...

CHAPTER 6

Marriage

I met my husband, Javonne Scott, during the summer of 1996 when the unit I was assigned to returned from providing security at the 1996 Olympics in Atlanta. I was 18 years old, and he was 23. It wasn't love at first sight. I wasn't thinking about a man or a relationship for that matter. Long before being raped, I said that I would never marry a man in the military. I didn't want that life. I knew I didn't join to be a lifer and I didn't want to be married to one. He was cool. We had a love/hate working relationship going on. As a matter of fact, the first time we met, we were both talking trash as if we had known each other for the longest time. He would aggravate me badly on a daily basis. I would later find out that he did that because he liked my smart mouth. He was and still is a trash talker and liked that I talked trash too. He says I was quick with my responses, and he liked that. Most people couldn't keep up with him in that area. In the military community, it's known that people hook up and it took no time for people to make assumptions about me and Jay. They just weren't true at that time. I was not interested in him in that way, and he was married when we first met. When I first met Jay, I was not looking for anyone. I was very untrusting of ALL men and was still ONLY dealing with them on my terms. I still wanted to be married and have a family, but it was definitely the furthest thing from my mind when arriving at Fort Stewart in the summer of 1996. Slowly, but surely, Jay was becoming my friend. He was someone that I could trust. I would talk to him about the guys I was dealing with. Our friendship blossomed and he would become one of my closest friends and confidants. Later that year, I found out I was pregnant, and Jay was the second person I told, only preceded by a cousin who was also stationed at Ft. Stewart during that time. Once I was pregnant and my commander was aware, she started the process to move me out of the barracks because I could no longer live there as a mother to be. I lived in a few different places before Javonne, and I became a couple. All of our mutual friends were saying that he and I were going to be together and neither one of us could see it. I never thought that he and I would end up together. He wasn't even my type. He was the opposite of what I said and thought I wanted. He wasn't tall, dark, and handsome like I preferred. Instead, he was handsome, but light skinned (lighter than me) and we were the same height 5'11". He was in the military and on track to do his 20. He was a soon to be divorcee and he was a father. So, with all those qualities that I didn't look for in a man, he was not on my radar at all. I never once looked at him sexually. However, I did notice that he was good looking, well-built and bow legged. I also took notice that a lot of the other girls in our unit and other units wanted him. I wasn't his type either. He preferred women shorter than him, and light skinned.

Your girl had options and with him being one of my best friends, I never thought about a future with him. We would talk about everything, especially the men I was dealing with to include my sperm donor. I never thought I would be in a relationship, let alone married to Jay. It never crossed my mind until it happened. He and I bonded over our issues. He was having problems in his marriage which was heading for separation and eventually divorce. I was dealing with my issues from being raped. I can't tell you when it happened, but we went from being friends, to being lovers, to being in a relationship and we never really had a dating period. We weren't together long before he proposed marriage on his birthday, December 31st on River Street in Savannah, GA. The proposal almost didn't happen because I was cold, tired, and ruining his plans for us for that night. He ended up proposing to me in the car. I often joke with him that I needed a do over. It would take 5 years for us to get married. I wanted to be his wife when I accepted his proposal, but I was not ready to be anyone's wife. I was still new to parenting and trying to figure out my next steps in life. We were already living together. Although it went against my upbringing, I was ok with us doing this. It was working for us, and I had to do what made me happy. I had to be in control of my decisions in my relationship. We endured being separated early in the relationship when he was stationed in Korea for a year. While he was there, we experienced the loss of our first child together. Neither of us knew that I was pregnant when he left and only learned of my pregnancy during my miscarriage. That grief coupled with other issues led to our first dealings with infidelity. He cheated on me and had a child with another woman. After he returned to the states, we broke up for a short period of time and eventually got back together. Our love for one another was undeniable and as badly as his betrayal hurt me, we found our way back to each other. He was still the safest place that I knew. I didn't want to lose him, and he didn't want to lose me. I will spare you the details of what led to the infidelity and how we ended back together but I will tell you that our love today is unbreakable. If you didn't know about all the things we have endured in this relationship, all you would know is what you see and that is the beautiful, happy marriage that we built. We have been together for 25 years and will celebrate 20 years of marriage on December 31, 2022. Jay was the first person that I talked to about being raped and the last two rapes happened during our relationship. He has been the only person in my life to know about these incidents for many years. He has been my main source of support and strength. He has been my safe place and my protector. I feel safest with him. He has been my strength at my weakest moments and my biggest cheerleader. He loves and accepts me for me.

He's patient and understanding and he deals with everything that comes with being with a woman like me. Someone may be thinking, you say all that, but he cheated on you. Yes, he did and I use to be of the belief that once a cheater, always a cheater but he has proven me wrong. He has been faithful ever since and I don't worry about whether it would or could happen again. I am confident in the fact that I know my husband and that he will never do that again. If I had any doubts, I would be gone. During our relationship, Jay was deployed 4 times. He was deployed to the Iraq War in 2003 two days after our courthouse wedding. I had just turned 25 on the 19th of December. I still wasn't ready to be married but he wanted to make sure that I was his wife before he left just in case, he didn't make it back.

Let's fast forward to 2006 - 2007 when I cheated... I had an affair and although I know that I will never do it again, I have come to the realization as to why and what led me to doing this. Not being healed from my trauma of sexual abuse, I was still very much struggling with my sexuality as well as my self-esteem and self-acceptance.

See, what I know now that I didn't know then,

was that I was still dealing with hyper sexuality and promiscuity. I disconnected from my body although I made the decision to get married. Pretending to be okay and failing to get help to heal, I allowed myself to be seduced by someone who wasn't my husband.

I cheated on my husband for multiple reasons. I was still hurting from him cheating on me during our dating/engagement period. I was still hurting from him getting her pregnant and me having lost our child to miscarriage. I told him that I had forgiven him. I said the words and I meant them when I said it. Honestly, I believed that I had forgiven him and moved past the hurt, but obviously I hadn't completely forgiven him and had been lying to myself. He cheated and it hurt. Because I had not completely dealt with that and totally left my trauma issues unaddressed, I, in turn cheated to make him feel that same hurt. If hurt people, hurt people was a person, it was me during that period. While Jay was doing what he was doing unknown to me, it transpired during the time I miscarried our child. That hurt, coupled with my trauma and no healing, left me in a vulnerable, mental space. I often did reckless things and made bad decisions. I was in self sabotage mode.

I won't say that I regret my actions because I own them. I am not ashamed of them. I DID IT! I hold my self accountable for my decision to be unfaithful in my marriage. I will say that when I made the decision to cheat, in my mind, our relationship was over. I know some of you may be reading this saying, well why not just leave and be done instead of cheating? I honestly can't answer why I didn't go that route. I can't explain how my brain was processing things during that time in my life. I can say I was still very hurt and upset and believe that wanting him to hurt like I did was a driving force in my decision process. I told my husband about the affair, assuming that he would divorce me, but he didn't. He told me that he always expected that something like this could and would happen because of what he had done. Of course, he would have rather I did not do it. I once believed in the saying once a cheater, always a cheater. However, I don't subscribe to that way of thinking anymore; at least not as it pertains to my marriage. Yes, he cheated once during our dating phase and in turn I cheated once early in our marriage. After my infidelity, we took the necessary time to get marriage counseling and therapy. We had much needed conversations and worked on ourselves and our marriage while remaining together. Our love and devotion to each other is greater, after all that we put each other through, than it was when we first began. We recommitted ourselves to one another and we both put in the work in our marriage.

When it first came out, I was treated like the black sheep at church while the man that I slept with was elevated and put on a pedestal. It was made to look as if I was some Jezebel who had seduced him and he didn't consciously make a choice. The affair came out because I wanted it to. I was tired of lying and hiding. I no longer cared about what the outcome of this affair becoming public would be. So, I told the one person that I knew would go run their mouth and she did just that. The news spread through the church like a wildfire through a forest of trees. People began showing their true colors towards me. It was no longer about the love of God and forgiveness because we all fall short daily. Due to people gossiping, the news soon hit the lead church in our District. People who I once considered to be "friends", took sides although I had not wronged them. It became about attempting to "slut" shame me while acting like he wasn't a fully willing participant. Little did they know, that man pursued me and was still pursuing me even after the affair was aired. Needless to say, once the "leaders" of the church started acting funny towards me, it soured me on the church for a long time.

Before the affair was aired, he told my father about us. I assumed he thought my father could influence me to leave my husband and be with him because he professed his love for me. He told me and my father that he loved me, he was in love with me and how I was the best he had ever had. I can't lie and say it wasn't a little ego booster to someone who had no confidence after all I had been through. The lack of self-worth and self-confidence coupled with unaddressed trauma will have you out here living reckless. As a Christian, it bothered me that one party could be treated as an outcast while the other party could be continually elevated in the church. Don't get me wrong. As a Christian, I believe in God's forgiveness and using His children in the kingdom as He sees fit, but I couldn't understand it. This man was in the pulpit like nothing happened.

If I remained at that church, I would have been sat down and no longer allowed to "serve" on the praise and worship team or sing in the choir. I felt like as he was being elevated by God and I was being punished. People often talk about the girl being "fast" for sleeping around, but they rarely know the reason behind that woman's actions. I am thankful that I stopped caring about what people had to say about me or their thoughts concerning me or my actions. It is not my concern or even my business what others say or feel about me. This is one of the key reasons why I am able to speak so freely and why I had no issue revealing this.

Over the years, my decreased self-esteem and self-worth had me with thoughts of whether I was only with Jay because he was safe. Was that the only reason why I loved him? I can now confidently say that this is not the case. Is it one of the reasons? Absolutely! Being in a relationship was the furthest thought from my mind. I was only dealing with men with a long-handled spoon including whatever man I was currently having sex with. Javonne had become a friend and proved to be someone that I could trust. He soon became the man that I undoubtedly could rely on. He has remained a safe place for me. I find safety in his arms, in his embrace, and in the way that he cares for me. I love the way that he covers me in prayer, protects me and deals with me. I'm ALOT to handle. I am not for the weak. I am happy that my husband loves me especially since I know that it isn't the easiest thing to do.

One of my daily devotions is "Lord, help me to be the best wife and mother. I refuse to fail in these areas of my life. My husband and children deserve the best of me, and I strive to always give it to them."

CHAPTER 7

Infertility

I have had 3 miscarriages. My 1st miscarriage was in 1998 and it was devastating. They all were. Each time I had a miscarriage, I was alone. Jay was either deployed, stationed in another country or we were living in a different state during the loss. During the 1st miscarriage, Jay was stationed in Korea. He was there for a couple of months when it happened, and we didn't even know that I was pregnant. As a matter of fact, at the time of each miscarriage, I was not aware that I was pregnant until I miscarried. That day had gone on like any other uneventful day. I had gone to work, and I was home in the bathroom. It was a Friday, and I was contemplating going to the club. I was using the bathroom and felt a pain in my stomach unlike anything that I had felt before. I also felt pressure in my vagina, and I knew it wasn't just urine. I was afraid to look and see what it was but when I did, I was horrified. I didn't know exactly what I was looking at, but I knew that it wasn't good. I called my grandmother who had been a nurse and she told me that it sounds like I had a miscarriage. I didn't think it was possible. How could that be? I wasn't pregnant. I was in shock. I got in the shower and cried. When I finished my shower, I called my best friend, Stephanie and went to the club. I went to the doctor the next day and was given an examination. It was determined that a D&C would not be required. They gave me a transvaginal ultrasound and confirmed that I had what they called a complete miscarriage and told me that I was 2 months along. Since I passed all the tissue, the D&C was not necessary. I called Jay later and told him. He was in Korea. Due to the 12-hour time difference, I had to wait until I would be able to talk to him. He didn't take the news well. We cried together on the phone over the loss of our 1st child together that until the day prior, we didn't know existed.

My 2nd miscarriage happened during one of Jay's deployments in the year 2000 just like the previous miscarriage. I was unaware that I was pregnant until I lost the baby. This would be the first time that I would undergo a dilation and curettage procedure better known as a D&C. Similar to the first miscarriage, I experienced bleeding and lots of cramping following the loss.

My 3rd miscarriage took place in 2008 while I was living in Wilson, NC with Jay's sister Tammy. This was prior to our relocation to Illinois. Jay had already relocated there but Destenee and I were still in South Carolina because I was still enrolled in school at the local college. We decided that I would move in with her and I would make the drive from Wilson, NC to Myrtle Beach, SC for class. I got an Office manager position at the new Bed Bath and Beyond that they had just built in Wilson and would remain there until I finished and then we would join Jay in Illinois. Again, I had no idea I was pregnant. It had been years since the prior two miscarriages and there had been no other pregnancies. I felt an all too familiar pain and had an all too familiar experience except. This time, there was so much blood - more blood than there had ever been. I called my sister-in-law, and she got me an appointment with her OB this time. They weren't able to absolutely confirm that it was indeed a miscarriage, but they were pretty sure that it was. I was sure as well especially from what I had experienced before. Again, an ultrasound was done. The miscarriage was confirmed but the D&C was not needed because there was nothing left. Between the 2nd and 3rd miscarriage, I had infrequent menstrual cycles. When I had them, it would vary from really heavy bleeding which I never had before. My cycle was now 3-5 days as oppose to the normal 7 days. I wasn't complaining about the shortened days and wasn't upset when my cycle didn't come at all.

In 2007, we moved to Illinois. I got established with an OB by the name of Dr. David Rawdon. I told him about my infrequent menstrual cycles and his response was that this was a problem. Being young and not knowing if you were having your menstrual cycle every month was an issue. I didn't mind that I wasn't having regular menstrual cycles. I told him about the severe abdominal pain that I was having. When this pain would occur, I would bawl up in the fetal position and just cry. Nothing would bring me relief. I would go to the ER when I was in the military. They documented in my records that they thought that I had endometriosis but never tested me for it. To treat it, they only prescribed Motrin. When I went to civilian hospitals, they would give me stronger medications and over time I was prescribed narcotics. The narcotics helped best but it was all temporary relief. The one medication that worked the greatest was Dilaudid. Dilaudid is more potent than morphine. When I went to the ER and asked for it, I was given a side eye and some other form of pain relief. After they saw for themselves that what they were given me wasn't working, they would end up giving me the Dilaudid. Dr. Rawdon was the only doctor that decided to do a laparoscopy to find out what was going on with me when countless ultrasounds didn't really yield any results. That is when I was diagnosed with PCOS (polycystic ovarian syndrome). Dr. Rawdon also confirmed what my military records reflected that I indeed also had Endometriosis. Endometriosis is defined as a "painful disorder in which tissue that normally line the inside of your uterus grows outside your uterus. It most commonly involves your ovaries, fallopian tubes and the tissue lining your pelvis." PCOS is a "hormonal disorder that causes women to have infrequent or prolonged menstrual periods and, in my case, excess male hormone (androgen) levels".

Both Endometriosis and PCOS cause infertility.

My PCOS symptoms included irregular periods (I went an entire year without a period), facial hair growth, weight gain, male pattern baldness (hair thinning in the middle of my head), infertility and depression.

My endometriosis symptoms were painful periods when I had them and even when I didn't bleed but it was the time of the month that I should have had a cycle. I would experience pain while using the bathroom, whether it was urinating or a bowel movement. My cycles, when they resumed, became heavy. I would often soak super tampons and pads in record time. Having sex with my husband, at one time, was very painful. For a period of time, our sex life was almost non-existent.

I was prescribed Metformin to help because PCOS makes you pre-diabetic. By lowering your insulin level, metformin allows many women to have more normal cycles. In my case, that didn't happen. I still wasn't having regular cycles. For years, even while taking Metformin, I was only having a few cycles a year. I was told that I wasn't ovulating due to that. In November of 2009, I was hired by Citibank.

They had the best health insurance package I ever had from an employer since leaving the military. Hubby and I decided that we would research fertility treatments.

Wait a minute. Let me back up…..

We moved to Missouri a year after I got the job with Citibank. I started my care initially with one Fertility Specialist but didn't feel like he was moving at a pace that we desired. We transferred our care to SSM Health where my physician, Dr. Dion Fisher partnered with PARINTS (Positive Approaches Regarding INfertility TreatmentS) who managed all my fertility care. Becky Kubala and her staff at P.A.R.I.N.T.S were amazing and held my hand through the entire process. They provided spiritual and emotional support. It was a match made in heaven for me and Jay.

At first, the fertility process was exciting and fun. Our initial consultation was over an hour long and we were provided with a lot of information and educated. I left that appointment feeling hopeful that we would have a child. At times, the process was stressful. We were encouraged to have sex every other day during cycle days 10-20. This was to increase Jay's ejaculations. Having long periods of abstinence was not helpful to the conception process. With basically having to have sex on demand, Jay became frustrated which made me feel like he didn't want it as badly as I did. Then, we talked, and he reassured me that he did. Having a good line of communication is key and being willing to hear and understand your partner's point of view is essential especially during this process.

I went through several cycles of Intrauterine Insemination treatments (IUI). I was prescribed Clomid, which helped to induce ovulation since the infertility disorders caused me to not ovulate. I was also having to give myself what is referred to as an HCG trigger shot. Jay had to administer them because I hate needles and couldn't do it myself. The shot would cause multiple eggs to grow to a mature size for insemination. Along with prenatal vitamins, I took 81 mg of aspirin to improve the implantation process. Jay was told to take a multivitamin because sperm loves zinc and selenium. After ovulation, I would take 200mg progesterone capsules at bedtime after we had sex or after insemination. On implantation days, Jay would provide his sperm that would then be washed and concentrated before being placed in my uterus around the time my ovary released eggs to be fertilized. Then we would wait two weeks before taking a pregnancy test to see if the procedure was successful.

God blessed me with a job where the insurance paid for my fertility treatments. Although we had the blessing of amazing insurance for these treatments, we were about to give up after several unsuccessful fertility treatment cycles. On May 1, 2012, I messaged some of my female cousins requesting prayers for Jay and me as we were on our 3rd round of fertility treatments. I was on the verge of giving up. Little did we know that 8 months later January 2, 2013, I would be sending those same cousins another message with a picture of 2 pregnancy tests thanking them for praying and believing God with us. God had given us our promise, our son. It had been seven years since Promise was prophesied to us. Over the years, we were told by 3 different people on 3 different occasions that God was going to fulfill the promise that He made to us to give us a son. The last treatment cycle was scheduled to yield results on our 10th wedding anniversary. We decided that if this was another failed attempt, we would be done. That would have been the worst anniversary ever and we would never forget that disappointment. I woke up in the middle of the night (I honestly don't think we ever really went to sleep) and I took the first pregnancy test and didn't have to wait for the time the instructions listed. The results were instantaneous. It was POSITIVE. I screamed and cried. I ran in the room to Jay and we embraced and rejoiced. Then, I called my mom crying and she could hardly make out what I was saying. She was half sleep and didn't comprehend what I told her until hours later. I was happy but still in disbelief that the test was positive. I proceeded to take the other test from the box and had Jay go to the store to get more tests. I ended up taking 6 tests before he refused to buy anymore. My results would be further confirmed by my doctors with a urinalysis and blood test.

Our son, Javonne Pierre Scott Jr was born on August 18, 2013. We were told during the fertility treatment process that multiples were possible. Twins run in my family so we thought there was a good chance that I would end up pregnant with twins. I didn't. However, Javonne was soon joined by his sister, Cassandra Denise Nicole Scott on November 10, 2014. The doctors explained that I had been on fertility meds for a long time and they were still in my system. Almost 2 years later, Savannah Niylah Scott would arrive on July 2, 2016. None of the doctors could explain it. God had replaced every child we lost by giving us what we affectionately refer to as our tribe: LJ, Cassie and Vannah. I LOVE and adore my family.

CHAPTER 8

Therapy

I am going to therapy. Yes! That's right. Therapy is for us too. For too long in the Black community, mental health topics were and, in some cases, still are taboo. Black people wouldn't dare even mention therapy or going to talk to anyone about their personal business or issues. You can almost forget about it in the church community. You wouldn't dare speak about a therapist or counseling other than spiritual counseling with your Pastor. Most "church folk" would tell you to pray rather than suggest, in conjunction with prayer, to seek professional mental health help. Thankfully, we have made some strides in our communities and in our churches. It isn't so much of an unthinkable topic as it once was. It took me 23 years to begin the process of addressing what I had gone through and to begin the healing process. For so long, I thought that if I could forget and not think about it, that I would be ok. I have never been more wrong in my life. I began the process by filing a disability claim with the VA. My father drove me to the VA after seeing me in lots of physical pain, which upset him. He asked me why I hadn't gone to the VA. At the time, I wasn't aware that I could be seen at the VA, let alone receive benefits. I completed a little less than the four years that I enlisted for, but my discharge was Honorable, which did entitle me to benefits as well as care. Because of my anxiety and depression, I was diagnosed with PTSD. Through the process of filing the claim, I had to recount my rapes. Prior to this, I only shared my traumatic experiences with 1 person, my husband. As I began recalling these rapes, that I could see so vividly in my mind as I spoke, I felt like I was currently being violated all over again. Although my husband was aware that I had been raped, I never gave him all the details.

I began therapy back in 2018 and it was extremely hard and worst of all, I found it hard to connect with my VA appointed therapist. I went for a few sessions and started cancelling the appointments that were made. When my uncle passed away in September of that year, it triggered a level of depression that I hadn't experienced since the early 2000s. I didn't know, at the time, that his death triggered my trauma symptoms. It was later explained to me in therapy that although his death wasn't a rape, it was a traumatic event that activated the depression and anxiety I already had.

My husband told me that when I talked about my trauma, it was like I was speaking about it from the outside looking in. He said that I spoke in a monotone voice and without emotion. I realized that when recalling my trauma, I am in a dissociative state. I subconsciously protect myself because the feelings use to overwhelm me. I was in so much pain, speaking about the rapes with anyone would cause anguish and it would engulf me. I was not accustomed to talking about it with anyone except my husband and I only told him that one time. We would speak about it randomly when the trauma would trigger something. Other than that, I wasn't familiar with talking to anyone. Now here I was having to tell someone at the VA what happened to me so that I could get help. First, I had to tell someone so I could be evaluated to receive benefits for Military

Sexual Trauma. Then, I had to tell the first therapist, but she wouldn't be the person to handle my case. Instead of her documenting what was said, (maybe she did, and the new therapist didn't read it) I had to tell yet another person. Over the course of trying different types of therapy and many therapists, I had to repeat the telling of my trauma countless times. This caused me to initially quit going. I couldn't handle the immense pain I would feel every time I had to talk about it. I felt exposed and frightened. It seemed like my life was turned upside down. I felt like I was in a dryer spin cycle. I wanted to quit because, in my opinion, my life was better before therapy than it was after I began going. Having to relieve my trauma made me more withdrawn and bought about more anxiety, panic attacks and nightmares. I was more irritable and just wanted to be left alone, which isn't possible when you have 3 small children to raise and a husband. I began to neglect my family and stay in my room alone. I hardly left the house and lost several friends. When I did interact with my family, it would take nothing to set me off. Every little thing made me angry, and it would happen in 2.5 seconds. This became my number one reason for wanting to get help. I needed help to deal with the anger inside of me. I didn't want to keep yelling at my children. Normal people can tell their kids to clean their rooms or pick up their toys. For me, I had to scream it at the top of my lungs because I was always mad. I made many mistakes while raising our oldest daughter, Destenee, and didn't want a repeat of that.

I was told that I had to push through and feel what I was feeling but to not quit. That was easier said than done. I imagined that therapy would closely align with what I had seen portrayed in movies and on TV. Not the whole laying on the couch and spilling your guts but the speaking about what you wanted to discuss and getting guidance on how to learn coping skills while being heard sharing what you needed to get off your chest. Well, it was nothing like this. It would begin with me telling them about the rape that I thought was the most traumatic and just focusing on that one event. Then depending on which therapist I had seen, they would give their opinion about things not even related to what I had told them or relevant to my issues. Over the years, I have only been able to connect with one of my assigned therapists. She was the last person I was assigned to in Charleston, SC and she was amazing. I had to give her up when we relocated to Mississippi, and I haven't been able to find another therapist. So, I dug deeper in self-help. Finishing this book was part of my healing process. I feel like I still have LOTS of work to do. Trust me! I am going to doing it. What I have realized in this process is that while seeking help from a professional, I can help myself by taking steps to work on myself and use the skills I have gained from my therapy sessions. I also realized that therapy is basically someone else giving an opinion (as well as knowledge gained from training) on what you should do to help yourself. Every proven method doesn't work for everyone and all situations. I have tried various methods of therapy that the Veteran Affairs offers, and not all of them were for me. Some that were offered, I turned down because I didn't want to take part in those types of therapy sessions such as the group sessions. I didn't want to sit around with other women and swap trauma stories. I also didn't want to participate in the therapy that matched you with a buddy that would coerce me to go to locations that I had been avoiding. I didn't want to speed through the process either. I wanted to feel comfortable with the person

I was sharing my deepest, darkest secrets with while knowing that I could peel back the layers at a rate of speed that I was most comfortable with. I refused all male therapist because I am not comfortable with them. I preferred having a therapist who was also an African American because I thought that she would be more relatable. However, I found that my best match came in a Caucasian woman. I didn't want the therapist to be my friend, but I did want someone who was friendly and empathetic. I wanted and needed to deal with a human; someone with feelings not a robot spitting out statistics and using half or more of my sessions focusing on things such as suicide when I wasn't suicidal. I understand the importance of asking someone if they are and ensuring that a safety plan is in place. I was sure to always have one since in the past, I had dealt with suicidal thoughts as well as trying to commit suicide. In these instances, I did not find it advantageous for so much time to be consumed during sessions talking about suicide when it wasn't a factor. Don't get me wrong. Therapy is a wonderful tool to utilize especially when you find a great therapist. I wish Veterans Affairs would have allowed me to keep my therapist from Charleston, SC when I relocated to

Brandon, MS. All of our sessions were done via Zoom calls. Neither she nor I thought it mattered that we would be in different states if we were both willing to keep going. We were the only ones who thought that way. I am not giving up. I am still searching for a new therapist in the area, but I am seeking this help outside of Veterans Affairs. In the meantime, I continue to do the work

I had to learn to forgive myself and move past the self-blame. The feelings of guilt and shame were overwhelming. I spent a lot of time blaming myself for what happened to me. Therapy and medicine don't erase the feelings, but they help you to manage them. Learning coping skills will help you with the things that trigger you.

CHAPTER 9

Dreams and Nightmares

Have you ever woke up scared to death, thinking that you could die or even felt like you were dying? No? Well, be glad that you haven't. I have experienced that many times. I would have such vivid dreams of my rapes and nightmares of other men trying to attack me. In some of my nightmares, those men were also trying to kill me. I would be fighting and crying in my dream and when I would get awakened by my husband or awake myself, I would be crying in real life. Those nightmares were so real to me. I would stay up for days not wanting to sleep so that I could feel safe. Then, it got to the point where I just couldn't sleep because of my PTSD symptoms. Most times, I could not see the face of my attackers, and this made me even more fearful of being around men, especially strangers. I started ensuring that I was never alone with any man.

Sometimes, I have intrusive memories of each of my rapes as well as unwanted dreams and/or nightmares about them. These recurring thoughts can be very distressing. It is like I am in the moment all over again. It has caused me severe emotional distress and more times than not, I have a physical reaction anytime something reminds me of any of my traumatic events. I tried to forget but I was still being haunted by the invasive, unwanted memories. At one point, I had become withdrawn. I began isolating myself even more and my depression got worse. On January 29th, 2020, my husband Jay, and I were making love and it was going great. Out of no-where, when he changed positions, I flashed back, and it was like I was back in the moment of one of my rape encounters. It felt like I was experiencing that rape all over again. I asked him to stop, and I ran to the bathroom. I began having a panic attack while showering. Jay got in the shower with me. I was bawling uncontrollably and almost passed out. He caught me and held me tightly. He told me, "I got you".

I would sometimes have nightmares while being wide awake. I didn't think it was possible until

I began experiencing them. I don't know what they are called. For me, that isn't necessarily important. I just wanted them to stop. I assumed something either in my environment or a sudden flashback caused them.

Even years after being in therapy, I still don't sleep much, and the nightmares still occur. The difference is that I allow myself to feel the emotions. One of the things that I learned during therapy is that I can't keep trying to avoid the feelings: the bad and ugly of it all. During the writing of this book, I would still have panic attacks. I chose to use some of the things I learned in therapy. I would take slow deep breaths while closing my eyes. I would focus on my breathing. I would focus my thoughts on something positive. If my husband and children were around, I would go to my husband and he would hold me until it passed. My children were good with hugging me and rubbing my back reassuringly without being aware of why I needed their embrace in that moment.

CHAPTER 10

Control

I must be in control. I have such anxiety when I am not, to the point that I often have panic attacks. If a situation arises where I feel like I am not in control, it makes me uncomfortable, irritable, and uneasy. I don't like the way it makes me feel. I don't feel safe. I found myself limiting my activity and changing around things in my life to fit so that I was always in control of my day before getting help.

The trauma I have suffered has caused a need to be in control of everything that happens in my life. One way I tried to assert control was by avoidance. I tried to avoid thinking about or even talking about rape. I don't go to places that remind me of any of my traumatic events. I also avoid some people and activities. This is something that didn't come about until after being raped but the level of control didn't kick in until much later. Oftentimes, I think. If I had the same level of needing to control back then that I have now, the 2nd and 3 rapes would not have occurred.

My affair began with flirting and inappropriate conversations. I will be honest. I liked the attention but most important to me was that I was in control of this situation. Every Sunday this man and I would find our way to each other during the part of the service where our Pastor would instruct us to greet one another, and we would hug. The attraction was strong and maybe it felt that way because we were doing something wrong. When he would walk past me, he would softly grab my waist and touch my butt. Here I was working and serving in the church and asking God to help me, but I failed to give up control.

I have negative thoughts about people. I can count on my hands the number of people I trust. I don't trust people, especially men. Outside of the men in my immediate family, I will not be left alone in a room with a man known or unknown to me. I am always on guard for danger and have taken steps to protect myself. I am never without protection. Most times, I don't feel safe. I am most safe at home with my children and husband.

I mainly spent my time at home in my bedroom. I spent most of my days since 2018 in isolation in my bedroom. I would attend church on Sundays and go to my parent's house for Sunday dinner afterwards. I would occasionally spend some time at my friend's beauty supply store, and I did go to work. I would only go somewhere if accompanied by my husband to include therapy. It had gotten so bad that I could not work because my anxiety felt a lot like paranoia. I was unable to control my surroundings in a place of employment and it became too overwhelming. I started calling out of work. Sometimes I, would even drive all the way there, sit in the parking lot, decide to call out and go back home. My anxiety would make me physically ill and exacerbate my physical pain. I am a hyper protective parent. I don't allow my children to go anywhere without me except for with the few people that I trust which are their grandparents, my or my husband siblings, and their godparents. My need to control got so bad that I didn't want them to go to school because I couldn't see them and know that they were safe. So, to address that, I became a substitute teacher and worked exclusively at their school. That way, I was in the building and felt closer to them. I was most at ease when subbing in their classes. Then, I became what is referred to as a floater. As a floater, I was no longer in just one classroom a day. I could walk around the school and assist in whatever capacity I was needed.

Unknowingly, my need to control seeped into every aspect of my life. My husband would tell me how I was trying to control him in many instances. I started seeking help in 2019 and started doing things for myself to help with my self-care. I had lost myself in the tunnel of despair. I was occupied with being a wife and mother. It seemed the harder I tried to do things for myself and to get help, the worse it got. There were many times that I needed and could have benefited from the help of others whether family or friends but I didn't want to be a burden to anyone. Instead, I suffered in silence for a long time. This was before coming to the realization that getting help and having someone to talk to was sometimes necessary and that therapy was vital to my well-being.

I kept trying to gain the lack of control I felt I

had over my situation. I realized that trying to control every aspect was actually hindering me from having control in the instances where I was the one in the driver's seat. I also realized that I am always in control of my day whether or not I can control the environment that I am in. I always have control over myself and my actions. I had to find the balance between things that I could control and those things that I wish that I could but couldn't. I still have anxiety during times when I cannot control an outcome or my surroundings but at least now I can cope better with that fact.

> **Gain control of your mind**
>
> **so that your mind doesn't control you.**
>
> **Control your mind = control your life.**

Practice self-care. It is ok to spend time alone. You need that time to recharge. Find balance and don't feel wrong for taking "me" time. I no longer feel guilty for needing time for myself. It is essential. In my family, we have built a dynamic for caring. My children understand when mommy needs that time to herself and when I need to recharge. If they can see that I am in physical pain, they are the first ones to tell me to go lay down or ask if I need to go to the hospital. For my son's birthday this year, he asked me to bake him some red velvet bundt cakes which are his favorite. Prior to his birthday, we went to the store to purchase what was needed for his birthday dinner and cake. He could tell that something was not quite right with me. Typically, they don't find me complaining about my issues or physical pain. He was able to recognize that something was wrong with me and he was concerned. In that moment, he no longer thought about himself and what he wanted. He opted to have chocolate chip cookies instead of having me bake his cake. He told me to spend the time I would have spent prepping, baking, and making the icing for his cake to rest. I had to hold back the waterworks in the store. My children constantly show me just how thoughtful and mindful of me that they are. They show me how much they care for me and love me. Because of the way that my husband cares for me and the way that we care for them, I am confident that my daughters know what it is to be well taken care of and they won't settle for less. My son is going to be a wonderful man and husband because he is already displaying some key qualities in his caring and thoughtful behavior.

CHAPTER 11

Pain in Multiple Forms (Physical/Mental/Social)

I suffer from all types of pain because of my traumatic rapes. People would tell me how strong I was without knowing all I had been through, all that I had done and was still doing to cope while trying to heal.

The military refers to what happened to me as MST (Military Sexual Trauma). This trauma has caused my diagnosis of PTSD. The pain that I experienced from Post-Traumatic Stress Disorder affect my life daily. I have issues with concentration in my daily life. I am all over the place. While writing this book, it was so hard to complete it because I would be on one section and would have a thought about something else. Then, I would go on a tangent getting the stuff together for that section of the book.

I have severe anxiety and suffer from panic attacks. Before therapy and learning ways to deal with the panic attacks, I experienced multiple on a daily basis. My mantra was I came, I saw, I had anxiety, so I left and this led me to doing less and spending more time in the house alone.

I suffer from the pain of not being able to maintain close relationships. I feel detached from others including my family and friends. I have lost many friendships due to my self-isolation. I believe that it was mainly due to me isolating myself and cutting myself away from others. It was also partly due to those same people choosing to not reach out even if I didn't. My thoughts were all over the place. I thought, if they were truly my friends and they noticed I was no longer reaching out, that they would reach out in return, but it didn't happen that way and I didn't have the capacity to care. They formed their opinions about me based on what would sometimes turn into negative interactions once I got frustrated with trying to convince them that they were not right about me.

You know - the worst part about being lonely is when you are surrounded by others, yet you still feel alone. It's great to talk about missing someone and wanting to spend time with them but when moments arise when it can be done even for just a little while, you choose to do something else. I didn't know if I should be angry, sad or both. I just dug deeper into my isolation and what I felt was my self-preservation. I had found myself over the years being loyal to people who weren't loyal to me. By isolating myself, I no longer had to worry about that.

I have lost interest in many things. I no longer enjoy activities that I once enjoyed doing. I used to be so outgoing and often called a people person. I have become content with being a homebody; spending my time at home with family that I created. Family time is sometimes painful because I am irritable a lot and have had lots of angry outbursts at my children. The smallest things send me from zero to 1000 in .02 seconds. My patience is slim to non-existent, which was one of the determining factors for me to continue going to therapy. I didn't want to be angry all the time and snap at my husband and children. I felt like I didn't have any control of my emotions which made me more upset because I must be in control all the time, yet I wasn't.

I struggle with experiencing positive emotions and that is one of the most painful things for me. I used to be such a happy people person. I have spent so much time being emotionally numb. It is all so exhausting.

A lot of the things that cause me mental pain are because I suffer from PTSD. The stress and anxiety cause me mental anguish and exacerbates my physical pain. The endometriosis led to me having to have a hysterectomy in July of 2021 to help relieve me of the pain being caused by this issue.

I spent years as a person with high functioning anxiety at work. I was detail-oriented, an overachiever, ambitious, driven, helpful, and organized. I took initiative, did my best work under pressure and was solution oriented. However, on the inside, I was overwhelmed, extremely self-critical, and always trying to please people. I over thought everything, had racing thoughts, focused on worst case scenarios, and fearful of failure. I found it very hard to say "no". I had unrealistic expectations. I was the ultimate procrastinator and always doing more. I lacked boundaries and experienced burn out. (UNKNOWN, 2022)

My depression and anxiety left me constantly tired, not wanting to eat; appetite just gone, wanting to stay in bed all day and many times, I did just that. I would make plans with people and cancel them. I would be happy and sad at the same time. I perpetually needed reassurance from my husband that I was beautiful, sexy and that he still wanted, desired and wasn't going to leave me. This often frustrated him because it understandably appeared as if I had doubts about his love, but that wasn't it at all.

As a survivor of rape, this battle with PTSD has been a constant battle of living with depression, anxiety, and panic attacks. It hasn't been easy for me. My anxiety over the years has been so bad that my life almost felt nonexistent. Gabriel Union said, "it shrinks your life" and I absolutely agree. I often still don't leave the house without my husband accompanying me. I am still filled with trepidation when things don't go as planned such as road construction causing me to have to take a detour. Panic attacks and anxiety can turn my anticipation about anything that I am excited about doing into complete misery.

CHAPTER 12

Healing/How I Made It

I am learning how to cope with what has happened. I am learning techniques to help me let go of all this anger that I have carried for so long. I'm optimistic that with intentional manifestation of the life that I want coupled with therapy, prayer, and God's help this will be life changing for me. I surround myself with positivity because these traumas have impacted me negatively long enough. I heard someone say "I don't have a sad story. God has been good to me…it ends in victory". I haven't gotten there yet, but it will end in victory. It is not the trauma that defines me but how I choose to move past it. I am coming out on the other side Victorious and not a Victim. I had to realize that it wasn't my fault. I was not the one to blame. I shouldn't feel ashamed. I didn't do anything wrong. I have learned that if it is not an implicit yes, then it is NO! This is whether I had flirted or teased him or not.

One day during a recent conversation with my best friend Sheena, she told me how she was a proud friend as I spoke to her about the small steps and progress that I was making. This included coming out of my room and taking steps to move forward with writing the book as well as the other things that I am doing to better myself. She said that I had pushed the button and helped myself along with having my support system but that I did it. I took a minute and thought to myself. The reality of it all is that yes, I had done it. I had to decide. Do I wallow in my situation and drown waiting for outside help from the VA and therapist (that was taking forever to come) or do I pick myself up and help myself the best way that I know how? I chose the latter. I was in denial for a long time thinking that I was handling it. It wasn't until 2019 that I realized not dealing with what happened to me, was making me worse. Pretending to be strong (not needing help) was also not effective. I was told by a beautiful, wise woman named Portia Prioleau that I was now in the place to not only receive the help, but for it to take root. Years later, I have opened up more. This has allowed me to meet some great people who otherwise I may not have met.

We need to stop associating strength with someone's ability to smile through tears while they are suffering in silence. Having courage enough to talk about what is hurting you is strength. For a long time, I had become good at smiling through the tears while suffering in silence. I was doing things and being strong and supportive for everyone else but myself. I was often told that I was such a strong person, but it just was not true. I had to find my strength. In my pain, strength was not optional. I had grown irritated and upset with constantly being told I was strong until I finally realized that I was. It took strength to speak about it. It took strength to talk about it. Those things didn't make me weak. Being a sufferer of depression and anxiety didn't make me weak. Having PTSD didn't weaken me. It just became a condition of my daily life that needed to be dealt with.

We must stop the stigma around depression. Lots of people think depression is caused by laziness, weakness, or someone's inability to just suck it up and deal with it. They couldn't be more wrong. Depression is caused by so many factors. Sexual trauma is just one of them. Depression is not always pill, bottles and suicide notes. Let's educate ourselves and check in on our family and friends, especially the "strong one". We must check on the ones who act goofy because they tend to be the ones who hide it the best. "The mere presence of at least one caring person doubles the endurance of an individual". Check on your people, even the strong ones. Depression isn't always displayed as sadness and crying. It is often cloaked in laughter and being the life of the party.

People, including family members, assumed because I was sleeping a lot and not doing things, that I was just being lazy. Not understanding that I was always exhausted from pretending that I was fine. I was exhausted from the constant battle going on in my head all day, every day. Sleep was one of the best ways to cope with my symptoms, avoid feelings and block out suicidal thoughts, rather than killing myself. It was also one of the prime symptoms of depression.

When I was having thoughts of suicide, one of the main reasons why I didn't follow through......

was my children. Sometimes, Savannah is scared at night and cries for me. It breaks me down. Knowing that she would cry like that nightly if I was no longer here, breaks my heart. I couldn't hurt them like that. My children saved my life. Despite often feeling like I am the worst mother, my children's selflessness reassures me that I mean the world to them.

When I was younger, I said as an adult that I wanted to be able to help other people. I thought of various ways in which I could do that. I didn't consider that the cost of that desire would mean that I would have to endure problems of my own. "I am courageously imperfect. I am beautifully broken. Still, I am an unstoppable force." (Sarah Jakes Roberts)

A friend, Sarena, posed a question one day asking, "if you could liken the most difficult trial of your life to any ball used in any sport, which ball would you choose?" She said "imagine what the ball endures, that might help you with your answer."

I responded, "a hockey puck".

Her response was "wow, the visual. Hockey Pucks gets whacked from every direction at times but the ice beneath them supports their ability to glide pass smoothly. Hadn't thought of that one. I like that sis. I appreciate that input".

In return I responded, no, thank you because I didn't think about the ice aiding the puck in gliding and sliding past. All I thought about was how the puck gets whacked from every direction as it pertains to my life. Instead of just looking at that, I should have looked at how as the ice helps the puck, God has helped me through all the whacks."

Sarena has a way with words. I found myself getting lots of encouragement directly through our conversations and indirectly from her social media posts. On another occasion, she made a post that said, "Thank you. Thank you for your bold light, tested resilience, and beautiful heart. We're living in a world and in times when the darkness bullies and threatens every day. But I look forward to seeing you because your vibe is so refreshing. If you're wondering who I'm talking to, it's you. I'm glad you're still here..." I needed to read that message on that day, and I loved the post but didn't comment. She reached out to me and said "I'm glad you recognized yourself in this! The story of your journey is a profound testimony that will surely give others a life raft in their turbulent waters. Truly you are beautiful inside and out." I was in a deep, dark place back in July 2020 when she wrote this. I thanked her for her constant encouragement and support and told her that her words are very uplifting and how much I appreciated her. Sarena Chipman James is one of the reasons I even followed through with writing a book.

On November 26, 2019, at the church I attended, I was asked to be one of the four speakers for our Thanksgiving program entitled "Almost Gave Up, But I Changed My Mind, Thankful That I Didn't...God Kept Me!" The purpose of this event was to address suicide in young adults. I was the last person to go, and I was afraid to share my story, but I did anyway. I told the listening audience about my trauma and how it affected my life. I told them about going to therapy and asked for their support and prayers. I had no idea or thoughts about what I had planned to share helping anyone other than to speak about my experience with suicide. Sharing my story was really for me. I could finally say the words out loud. Getting up there and speaking about my trauma was more for me just like writing of this book. If I can help someone, that would be amazing. I would be so happy about that but in writing this book, I was trying to help myself heal. When I was done speaking that night, I was approached by several women who began sharing their stories with me. I was told repeatedly from various people how my story would help those who would hear it. Sarena approached me after that program. Both of us were speakers. During that service, I openly shared my story for the first time (besides telling my husband and therapy). This would be the first time that my parents would hear about what transpired during my time in the Army and why I decided to get out of the Army.

Since first sharing my testimony, I have been told how powerful it is and how strong I am. I have to say I struggled with that. I did not see it as being strong. When I was told that they loved my testimony, it irritated me. My mind could not reconcile what was to love about my trauma. Did they love my pain? I know that no one meant anything negative but, in my mind, that's just how crazy my thoughts were.

Although I was no longer angry with God, I

was still very much angry with every man that violated me. Through a conversation with my mom, I was reminded that I needed to forgive them. This forgiveness was not for them but for me in an effort to continue healing myself. Another one of Sarena's posts was timely when this turning point began for me. The question posed was "If LOVE itself kept a journal, what would be ONE of the sentences it would write?" There were so many great responses. One person commented "I forgive you" as their response. That sparked an emotional reaction from myself as I made the correlation of the importance of forgiveness and love and how greatly they are intertwined. I needed to love and forgive myself and forgive those who traumatized me. Forgiveness is for you. It is essential for your healing and sometimes others reap the benefits. My response to the question posed was "I give it to you freely and unconditionally" to which Sarena replies "Sis!!! That one sentence is an ENTIRE book by itself! I hear your point. I had a conversation with someone who said love most certainly had conditions. And because of her experiences it made me cry. I'm not sure it was love she's ever had..." I don't want love given with conditions attached. When I love, I do it whole heartedly and desire the same in return, yet I understand that some people are incapable of doing this.

One Sunday, Evangelist Ena Binns was preaching at the church I attended. I felt like she was speaking directly to me. I was that person at church with the fake smile attempting to praise God when all I wanted to do was lay in my bed and cry from the physical, mental, and emotional pain that I was enduring. This is something that I had done on many occasions. That day, her message was uplifting and encouraging and despite all the previous messages I heard, hers got through to me. Although I left feeling encouraged, my depression was not gone. I didn't receive any instant deliverance from the suffering of PTSD and anxiety. I was still depressed. I was still anxious and stressed. I was still in pain mentally and physically, but the seed had been planted so that healing could begin to take place. What had taken place was not visible to the human eye. It wasn't even visible to me. I still couldn't see past my current state of being. I just knew I wanted to be better. I wanted to heal. I wanted help and I continued to seek for it. I slowly started doing things for my self-care. During the time when I was alone in my room, I read my Bible. I read Ferocious Warrior and I read a book by my friend, Danielle Lee-Hodges entitled, "Shame Is Not The Blame: How Overcoming Pain Leads to Purpose". Still yet, the healing was not instantaneous. I went through some of my darkest days after I made up my mind that things would be different. The harder I fought, the darker my days became, but I didn't give up. I continued working on me, going to therapy, and speaking and writing affirmations for myself. My Pastor and First Lady, Bishop William and First Lady Ena Prioleau, called to see about me. They also shared scriptures and praying for and with me.

There were many others who unknowingly and purposefully encouraged me and spoke to me. I have received some of the best advice, insight and encouraging words from various sources. From Facebook "friends" who don't even know what I am going through but felt compelled to reach out. From a few friends who are aware and wanted to see me better. From my mommy who is always available with a listening ear when I wanted or needed to talk but she never pressed me. She disagreed with how I often chose to cope. Rather than beat me down, she would try to get through to me. Most importantly, she would just pray.

My biggest supporter through all of this has been and remains to be my husband of 20 years, Javonne Scott and my children. Throughout this healing process my husband has carried this family. There were many days when I couldn't or wouldn't get out of bed and he took care of me, the household, and our children. My children support me in ways that they don't even realize. Jay and I joke about how we prayed for one child, but God gave us three and how we would have been ok with just having that one child. We have come to realize that I needed the three. Javonne Jr. (LJ) my son is a gentle soul who love his momma and my Promise. Cassandra, affectionately known as momma Cassie, makes sure her mommy is good. She takes care of me and is one of my protectors. That last one, Savannah! God knew I needed her. She came at a time when I was dealing with not being able to walk or stand upright due to back issues as well as some other health issues that arose from having Endometriosis and PCOS. I had to stop breast feeding Savannah earlier than my other three children because of my pain issues and needing to take narcotics for pain management. She and I spent a lot of time together, chest to chest. Although we slept with all of our children, she stayed with us the longest. She still comes to get in the bed with us and has told her father many times that it was her bed. She encourages me the most and has done so since she could talk. I feel like she is the child that is most connected to me. Every time I think about past times when I was really depressed or on the days when the pain was the worst, it was like she was keenly in tune with what was going on with me and would not leave my side. My children and husband rally together whenever the pain overwhelms me, or I am unable to do things. They are always right there. They have given me strength and courage to go on. On the days that I didn't want to do it for me, I did it for them. They are my Why!

I've heard that survival takes strength and there is strength in vulnerability. I am finding both statements to be true. I aspired to be completely vulnerable throughout this writing process. I was gifted a book entitled, "Ferocious Warrior" by Cora Jakes Coleman. The person who sent me the book told me that I was stronger than I think. She was right. One thing I have realized is that I am a lot stronger than I have ever given myself credit for. I had to remind myself to breathe. This is just a chapter in my life, not my entire story.

Accept that it hurt you. Expect it to change you. Refuse to let it define you, deter you or reduce you. Take depression and turn it around to "I pressed on". I am winning and it isn't pretty. I want you to let go of something that you have been holding on to that serves no benefit to you. It can be hurt, guilt, shame, anger. Whatever it is, let it Go! Your life is much more than that single chapter that is keeping you from exhaling.

Healing for me has been quite the journey. I heard someone say that "God knows how to do wonderful things suddenly." That may be true but there are some things that God does eventually. My healing has been an eventual process, not a sudden one. Whether God chooses to do it suddenly or eventually, my praise must be continual. As I wrote this book and walked through this healing process, I didn't know where God was leading me. You may not know where He is leading you, but just know that He won't lead you astray. It will always be to a destination better than where you would have led yourself. If you cannot understand why someone's grief or healing process is taking so long, consider yourself lucky that you don't understand.

I have spent so much time and energy trying to forget about my trauma until I started getting help. I came across a Facebook post from a therapist that stated "I do not have to 'get over' things to keep going. I can continue despite what has happened to me without trying to forget." (TAWWAB, 2020). It hurt me, but it didn't destroy me!

I AM NOT ALONE IN THIS!
AND NEITHER ARE YOU!

Get help. Have someone to be accountable to. Grant them permission to check on you whether you have taken your meds or have gone to therapy. Just be accountable to someone other than yourself to help you through the healing process. Your mental health is important and if you think it isn't impacted by traumatic events, you are mistaken. Whether it is depression, anxiety, PTSD, suicidal thoughts, or all of them together, you need to seek help from professionals. Talk to your family or a trusted friend. Get help from someone that you can rely on and get a treatment plan in place. Focus on yourself. Give yourself the grace, help and attention you would give someone else.

In giving my self-grace, I had to be real with myself. There is a saying that states "if you can't be positive at least be quiet". I had to apply that to my own situation. If I couldn't speak positively to myself about myself, I needed to shut up. I couldn't solely depend on affirmation and positivity from others. I had to pour into myself. I had to build up myself. I was reminded of something I learned as a teenager. Attitudes are contagious. Is yours worth catching? Many days my attitude towards myself were piss poor. I would treat others with respect but show myself little to none. I forgot that my words as well as my negative thoughts had power. I was supplying the wrong energy and speaking the wrong words to myself. I needed to correct that ASAP. Once you change how you view and value yourself, you will think differently. You will speak differently, and you will operate differently.

If given medicine, don't look at it as a bad thing. Take your meds. If you are a person of faith and you think getting help means that you don't have faith in God, dismiss those thoughts. You going to therapy or taking meds to help with your mental health does not negate your belief in God. Like me, you may feel that you didn't pray enough, that you didn't read your Bible enough or that you were being punished for some reason. Some believers feel that if they can't pray their way through a situation that their faith isn't strong enough. There are areas in my life where my faith is stronger. I pray and ask God for help in the areas where my faith needs to be built up. I know that me seeking help didn't diminish my faith or trust in God. I realized that I needed all of those things. It wasn't my lack of prayer or trying. I have an issue that I cannot manage without help!

You don't have to feel ashamed that you need medication to help you with depression and or anxiety. You have an issue that needs help. If you pray, keep doing that. Keep reading your Bible. In addition to trusting and believing God, use wisdom and seek professional help.

I'm Chennetta Scott And I'm A Survivor!

From now on...

I will speak Freedom

I declare that I am Free

Free from the bondage of

Anger

Shame and guilt

Despair

Anxiety, panic attacks and depression

Free from self-blame

Free from all hindrances

I'll go through it

I'll glow through it

I'll grow through it

Escape the past

Push on to the present

Ponder the possibilities

In my pain, the strength was not optional!

RESOURCES AND STATISTICS

An unfortunate fact is that sexual assault is prevalent in our military as well as in our communities. Lots of women have even suffered and lost their lives so that they couldn't tell what happened to them. Sexual assault doesn't only happen to women, men have been and are victims of it as well. I encourage all women and men alike to take up a self-defense course.

A 2011 report found that women in the U.S. military were more likely to be raped by fellow soldiers than they were to be killed in combat.

At a November 2011 press conference introducing legislation to combat sexual assault in the armed forces, Rep. Jackie Speier stated that of the 13% of military sexual assault victims who reported the crimes committed against them, 90% were involuntarily discharged.

In September 2013, Congress received the U.S. Commission on Civil Rights 2013 Statutory Enforcement

Report. The report found that during the 2012 fiscal year, there were 3,374 reports of sexual assault upon military service members. Of these, 816 were not included in the commission report because they were confidential, restricted, and not investigated. The report indicated that commanders are increasingly likely to refer sexual assault cases to court martial compared to the prior four years. In 15% of cases, the accused perpetrator was permitted to resign or be discharged in lieu of court martial.

The same commission report included the results of an anonymous survey of military personnel in which 23% of women and 4% of men reported experiencing unwanted sexual contact since enlistment. Based on this survey, the Department of Defense estimated that 26,000 service members experienced some form of unwanted sexual contact, from groping to rape, in the year 2012. 34% of women and 24% of men who reported these events in the anonymous survey stated that they had reported the event to authorities.

According to a 2013 United States Commission on Civil Rights report, a 2010 survey conducted by the Department of Defense found that 54% of women and 27% of men did not report incidents because they feared retaliation; the survey also found that 47% of women and 20% of men did not report incidents because they had heard other victims had a negative experience after reporting.

https://en.wikipedia.org/wiki/Sexual_assault_in_the_United_States_military#cite_note-ABC_News-18)

According to the CDC - https://www.cdc.gov/injury/features/sexual-violence

- Nearly 1 in 5 women have experienced completed or attempted rape during their lifetime.

- 1 in 3 female rape victims experienced it for the first time between 11-17 years old.

- 1 in 8 female rape victims reported that it occurred before age 10.

- Nearly 1 in 38 men have experienced completed or attempted rape during their lifetime.

- About 1 in 4 male rape victims experienced it for the first time between 11-17 years old.

- About 1 in 4 male rape victims reported that

it occurred before age 10.

Seek therapy and begin a self- care routine.

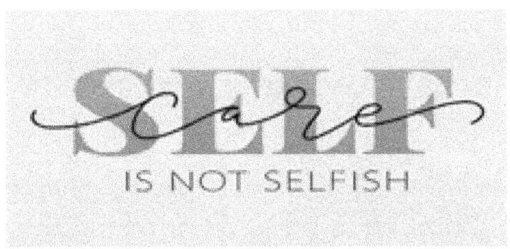

Your mental health is important. Your happiness is crucial, and self-care is a requirement.

Adapted from: @lauraheartlines

https://freshyouth.org/self-care

ABOUT THE AUTHOR

Chennetta Renae

Chennetta Renae Scott is a no-nonsense passionate woman from Paterson, NJ and has lived in various states since moving to South Carolina as a child. She is the oldest of five and a mother of four beautiful children: three daughters (Destenee, Cassandra, and Savannah) and 1 son (Javonne Jr.) She has been happily married for 20 years (December 21,2022) to the love of her life, Javonne Scott.

After serving in the Army, Chennetta went on to work in the accounting and banking industry fields. She has spent the last 4 years working in Education starting as a substitute teacher to now working as a school secretary to be active in the school district where her children attend school. In her spare time, she loves baking, spending quality time with her family, and playing the PC version of The Sims. Chennetta especially loves travelling with her husband.

She is an author and public speaker with a message of hope, overcoming and complete victory.